P9-DMC-133

DISCARDED
from
New Hanover County Public Library

# Solids, Liquids, and Gases Experiments
# Using Water, Air, Marbles, and More

## One Hour or Less Science Experiments

## ROBERT GARDNER

New Hanover County Public Library
201 Chestnut Street
Wilmington, North Carolina 28401

**Enslow Publishers, Inc.**
40 Industrial Road
Box 398
Berkeley Heights, NJ 07922
USA

http://www.enslow.com

Copyright © 2013 by Robert Gardner

All rights reserved.

No part of this book may be reproduced by any means without the written permission of the publisher.

Library of Congress Cataloging-in-Publication Data

Gardner, Robert, 1929–
  Solids, liquids, and gases experiments using water, air, marbles, and more : one hour or less science experiments / Robert Gardner.
      p. cm. — (Last-minute science projects)
  Summary: "Provides simple experiments to learn about the changing states of matter, density, viscosity, and the conduction of electricity by solids"— Provided by publisher.
  Includes index.
  ISBN 978-0-7660-3962-9
  1. Change of state (Physics)—Experiments—Juvenile literature. 2. Science—Experiments—Juvenile literature.  I. Title.
   QC301.G37 2012
   530.078—dc23
                              2011019957

Future editions:
Paperback ISBN 978-1-4644-0143-5
ePUB ISBN 978-1-4645-1050-2
PDF ISBN 978-1-4646-1050-9

Printed in the United States of America

042012 Lake Book Manufacturing, Inc., Melrose Park, IL

10 9 8 7 6 5 4 3 2 1

To Our Readers: We have done our best to make sure all Internet Addresses in this book were active and appropriate when we went to press. However, the author and the publisher have no control over and assume no liability for the material available on those Internet sites or on other Web sites they may link to. Any comments or suggestions can be sent by e-mail to comments@enslow.com or to the address on the back cover.

♻ Enslow Publishers, Inc., is committed to printing our books on recycled paper. The paper in every book contains 10% to 30% post-consumer waste (PCW). The cover board on the outside of each book contains 100% PCW. Our goal is to do our part to help young people and the environment too!

Illustration Credits: © 2012 by Stephen Rountree (www.rountreegraphics.com), pp. 13, 15, 17, 19 (marbles), 21, 23, 29, 31, 33 (b), 35, 37, 41, 43; Enslow Publishers, Inc., p. 33 (c);  Jonathan Moreno, p. 11 (c); Andrew Lambert Photography/Photo Researchers, Inc., p. 33 (a); Shutterstock.com, pp. 1, 3, 39 (b); Stephen F. Delisle, pp. 9, 27; Tom LaBaff and Stephanie LaBaff, pp. 11 (a, b), 19 (cylinders), 25, 39 (a, c).

Cover Photos: Shutterstock.com

# Contents

DISCARDED
from
New Hanover County Public Library

🎖 Contains ideas for more science fair projects

# Are You Running Late?

Do you have a science project due tomorrow and you've put it off until now? This book provides a solution! Here you will find experiments with solids, liquids, and gases that you can do in one hour or less. In fact, some of them can be done in 30 minutes, others in 15 minutes, and some in as little as 5 minutes. Even if you have plenty of time to prepare for your next science project or science fair, or are just looking for some fun science experiments, you can enjoy this book, too.

Most of the experiments are followed by a "Keep Exploring" section. There you will find ideas for projects or experiments in which the details are left to you. You can design and carry out your own experiments, **under adult supervision**, when you have more time.

Sometimes you may need a partner. Work with someone who likes to experiment as much as you do so you will both have fun. **Please follow any safety warnings and work with an adult when it is suggested**.

This is a book about the three states of matter—solids, liquids, and gases. Scientists define matter as anything that has mass and occupies space. Mass is anything that resists motion. A mass at rest will not move unless a force acts on it. When a force does act on it, the mass accelerates. If there is no friction, the mass is equal to the force divided by the acceleration (mass = force/acceleration). The mass of a sample of matter can easily be measured on a balance. Small masses are measured in grams, large masses in kilograms.

# The Scientific Method

Different sciences use different ways of experimenting. Depending on the problem, one method is likely to be better than another. Designing a new medicine for heart disease and finding evidence of water on Mars require different experiments.

Even with these differences, most scientists use the scientific method. This includes: making an observation, coming up with a question, making a hypothesis (a possible answer to the question) and a prediction (an if-then statement), designing and conducting an experiment, analyzing results, drawing conclusions, and deciding if the hypothesis is true or false. Scientists share their results. They publish articles in science journals.

Once you have a question, you can make a hypothesis. Your hypothesis is a possible answer to the question (what you think will happen). For example, you might hypothesize that a gas will expand when heated. Then you test your hypothesis.

In most cases you should do a controlled experiment. This means having two groups that are treated the same except for the thing being tested. That thing is called a variable. For example, you might have two identical air-filled balloons. After measuring the volume of the balloons, you would place one balloon in a warm environment for a few minutes. You would then measure the volume of both balloons again. If the volume of the balloon in the warmer environment had increased while the volume of the other balloon was unchanged, you would conclude that your hypothesis is true.

The results of one experiment often lead to another question. Or they may send you off in another direction. Whatever the results, something can be learned from every experiment!

## Science Fairs

All of the investigations in this book contain ideas that might lead you to a science fair project. However, judges at science fairs do not reward projects or experiments that are simply copied from a book. For example, a diagram of a steam engine would not impress most judges; however, a balance made from a soda straw that could weigh the wing of a fly would attract their attention.

Science fair judges tend to reward creative thought and imagination. It is difficult to be creative or imaginative unless you are really interested in your project. Therefore, try to choose an investigation that excites you. And before you jump into a project, consider, too, your own talents and the cost of the materials you will need.

If you decide to use an experiment or idea found in this book for a science fair, find ways to modify or extend it. This should not be difficult. As you do investigations, you will get new ideas. You will think of questions that experiments can answer. The experiments will make great science fair projects because the ideas are your own and are interesting to you.

## Your Notebook

Your notebook, as any scientist will tell you, is a valuable possession. It should contain ideas you may have as you experiment, sketches you may draw, calculations you make, and hypotheses you may suggest. It should include a description of every experiment you do as well as the data you record (such as voltages, currents, resistors, weights, and so on). It should also contain the results of your experiments, graphs you draw, and any conclusions you may be able to reach based on your results.

# Safety First

1. Do any experiments or projects, whether from this book or of your own design, under the supervision of a science teacher or other knowledgeable adult.

2. Read all instructions carefully before proceeding with a project. If you have questions, check with your supervisor before going any further.

3. Always wear safety goggles when doing experiments that could cause particles to enter your eyes. Tie back long hair. Do not wear sandals.

4. Do not eat or drink while experimenting. Never taste substances being used (unless instructed to do so).

5. Do not touch chemicals, and do not let water drops fall on a hot lightbulb.

6. The liquid in some thermometers is mercury (a dense liquid metal). It is dangerous to touch mercury or breathe mercury vapor. Therefore, mercury thermometers have been banned in many states. In these experiments, use only non-mercury thermometers, such as those filled with alcohol. If you have a mercury thermometer, ask an adult if it can be taken to a local thermometer exchange location.

7. Do only those experiments that are described in the book or those that have been approved by an adult.

8. Maintain a serious attitude while conducting experiments. Never engage in horseplay or play practical jokes.

9. Remove all items not needed for the experiment from your work space.

10. At the end of every activity, clean all materials used and put them away. Then wash your hands thoroughly with soap and water.

# One Hour or Less

## 60 min

Here are experiments involving one or more of the three states of matter that you can do in one hour or less. You don't have any time to lose, so let's get started!

# 1 Three States of Matter: Solids, Liquids, and Gases

## What's the Plan?

Let's examine the three states of matter.

## What You Do

1. Examine a block of wood—a solid. As you can see, its shape and volume are fixed.

2. Examine water—a clear liquid. Pour some water into a glass. Then pour it into a pan. A liquid takes the shape of its container. If it doesn't evaporate, its volume doesn't change.

3. Examine air—a gas. Fill a balloon with air. You can change the gas's shape by squeezing the balloon. Let the air escape. It spreads throughout the room. It doesn't have a fixed volume.

4. Draw some air into a plastic syringe (Figure 1a). Put your finger firmly over the narrow end of the syringe. Then push the piston farther into the cylinder (Figure 1b). Your force changed the shape and volume of the gas.

**WHAT YOU NEED:**
- wood block
- water
- drinking glass
- pan
- balloon
- plastic syringe
- dry sand

**5.** Hold your finger tightly against the open end of the syringe. Push the piston in and then release it. The gas expands as the pressure on it is reduced.

**6.** Try the same thing with water. Draw some water into the syringe. Place your finger tightly against the open end of the cylinder. Try to push the piston inward. You'll find that liquids can't be compressed.

**7.** Half-fill a plastic syringe's cylinder with fine, dry sand. Put your finger over the open end. Try to push the piston into the cylinder. As you see, solids can't be compressed either.

## What's Going On?

As you have seen, a solid has a definite, unchanging shape and volume. A liquid has a fixed volume but its shape is determined by its container. A gas has neither a fixed shape nor volume. It can be compressed into a smaller volume or allowed to expand to fill any volume.

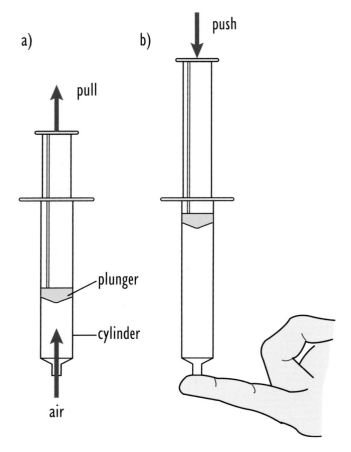

Figure I. a) Draw air into a cylinder by pulling the piston outward. b) Push the piston inward, squeezing the air into a smaller volume.

# 2 Conduction of Electricity by Solids

## What's the Plan?

Which solids conduct electricity?

## What You Do

1. If you have a bulb and battery holders, arrange the circuit as shown in Figure 2a. If you don't, attach the bare end of a wire to each pole (end) of a D-cell as shown in Figure 2b.

2. Wrap the end of one wire tightly around a flashlight bulb. Then tape it firmly in place.

3. Press the base of the bulb firmly against a side of the object being tested. Press the end of the free wire against the other side. If the bulb lights, the object conducts electricity. If it doesn't light, the object is a nonconductor, a poor conductor, or you haven't made a good connection.

4. Test a variety of solid objects—nails, silverware, coins, scissors, and other metallic things, as well as solids made of plastic, paper, glass, wood, cardboard, wax, and chalk. Record whether the objects conduct electricity.

**WHAT YOU NEED:**

- bulb and battery holders (optional)
- rubber band
- 2 paper clips
- 2 clothespins
- copper wires
- D-cell
- tape
- flashlight bulb
- solid objects listed in Step 4

## What's Going On?

Metals, as you probably found, are good conductors of electricity. Paper, plastic, glass, wood, cardboard, wax, and chalk are not good conductors.

## Keep Exploring—If You Have More Time!

- Can liquids conduct electricity? Use a 6-volt lantern battery in place of the D-cell (Figure 2c). Liquids tend not to conduct electricity as well as metals. Place a liquid in a plastic cup or vial. Slide two paper clips over the sides of the container and into the liquid. The lower half of each clip should be covered with liquid. Test different liquids such as water, vinegar, milk, fruit juices, and cooking oil, as well as solutions of salt and sugar.

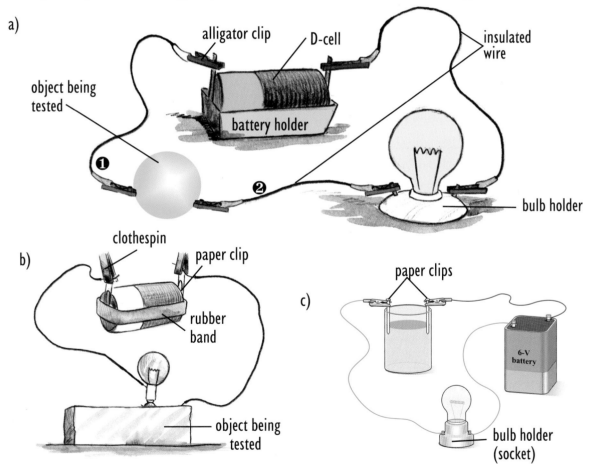

Figure 2. a) Testing for conductivity when battery and bulb holders are available as well as wires with alligator clips. b) Testing when battery and bulb holders are not available. c) Can liquids conduct electricity?

# 3 Thermal (Heat) Expansion of a Solid

## What's the Plan?

Does metal expand when heated?

## What You Do

**1.** Clamp the wide end of a hollow, metal knitting needle to a soft pine board (about 6 in x 1.5 in x 3/4 in) that extends from and is clamped to a bench or table (Figure 3).

**2.** Rest the other end of the knitting needle on a second identical board that extends from the same bench or table. That board should also be clamped to the bench or table. Place a large sewing needle under the free end of the knitting needle. The sewing needle should extend about an inch beyond the board (Figure 3 Overhead View).

**3.** Push the end of a vertical soda straw through the end of the sewing needle. If the knitting needle expands when heated, it will turn the sewing needle and the attached soda straw pointer.

**4.** Insert a map pin in the side of the second board. Wrap a rubber band around the

### WHAT YOU NEED:

- an adult
- metal knitting needle 12 to 14 in long with a diameter of 5/16 in
- 3 C-clamps
- 2 soft pine boards (about 6 in x 1.5 in x 3/4 in)
- bench or table
- large sewing needle
- ruler
- map pin
- rubber band
- soda straw
- matches
- 2 candles

pin and near the end of the knitting needle so that the knitting needle is pressed firmly against the sewing needle.

5. **Ask an adult** to light two candles and move the flames back and forth along the underside of the knitting needle. Watch the soda straw pointer as the temperature of the knitting needle increases.

6. Finally, remove the candles and watch the soda straw as the metal cools.

## What's Going On?

The metallic knitting needle expanded as its temperature increased. As it expanded, it turned the sewing needle on which it rested. As the sewing needle turned, so did the soda straw attached to it.

As the metal cooled, the knitting needle contracted to its original length and the soda straw returned to its initial position.

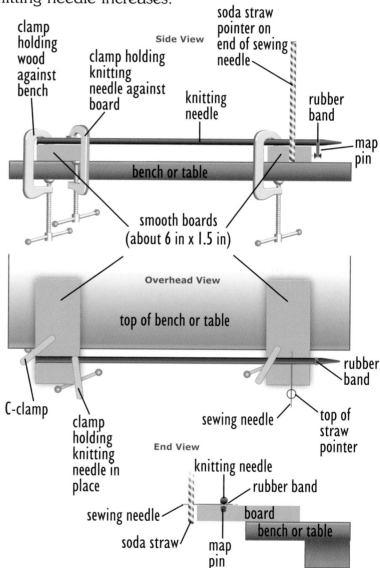

Figure 3. This apparatus used in an experiment to see if a metal expands when heated.

# 4 Estimating the Volume and Weight of Matter

## What's the Plan?

Let's estimate the volume and weight of some matter (an orange).

## What You Do

1. Find an orange's diameter using two sticks, such as coffee stirrers, and a metric ruler (Figure 4a).

2. Assume the orange is a sphere. Use half its diameter (radius) to estimate its volume. Remember: The volume of a sphere equals $4/3\ \pi r^3$. (Use 3.14 as the value of $\pi$.)

3. Check your estimate by displacing water. Put water in a metric measuring cup. Be sure you have enough water to submerge the orange. Record the water's volume.

4. Use a thin pointed object, such as a pencil, to keep the orange submerged (Figure 4b). Measure and record the total volume (water + orange). Subtract the volume of the water from the total volume to find the volume of the orange. How close was your estimate?

### WHAT YOU NEED:

- an orange
- 2 sticks, such as coffee stirrers
- metric ruler
- water
- metric measuring cup
- pen or pencil
- notebook
- thin pointed object, such as a pencil
- a balance

**5.** Archimedes' principle tells us that a floating object displaces a weight of water equal to its own weight. Water weighs one gram per milliliter. Measure the water displaced by the floating orange. Then estimate the orange's weight in grams.

**6.** Weigh the orange on a balance. How close was your estimate?

## What's Going On?

You can make reasonable estimates about matter's weight and volume without measuring either weight or volume. The author used an orange with an average diameter of 7.8 cm. Its estimated volume was $4/3 \pi (3.9)^3 = 4/3 \times 3.14 \times 59.3 \text{ cm}^3 = 248 \text{ cm}^3$. Its volume as measured by water displacement was 240 mL (440 mL – 200 mL) or 240 cm³ because 1 cm³ = 1 mL. Its estimated weight was 215 g because it displaced 215 mL of water. On a balance it weighed 219 g.

## Keep Exploring—If You Have More Time!

- Estimate the mass and volume of an object that sinks in water.

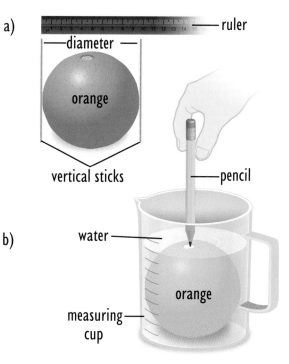

Figure 4. a) Assume an orange is a sphere. Estimate its volume. b) Measure the orange's volume by displacing water. The orange will displace a volume equal to its own volume.

# 5 Viscosity (Thickness)

## What's the Plan?

Let's look for frictional forces in liquids—a property known as viscosity or thickness.

## What You Do

1. Use a small nail to make a hole in the bottom of a foam cup. To do so, put the nail inside the cup. Gently push it through the center of the bottom, then remove it.

2. Hold your finger over the hole while you fill the cup to a readily identifiable level with tap water at room temperature.

3. Have a partner with a stopwatch that can measure seconds say "Go!" When you hear "Go," remove your finger. Let the water empty into a second cup in a sink (Figure 5). At the moment the water stops flowing from the cup, say "Stop!"

4. When she hears "Stop!" your partner should stop the watch and record the time that has elapsed since timing started.

5. Repeat the experiment several times to be sure your results are reasonably consistent. Then calculate and record the average time for water to empty from the cup.

### WHAT YOU NEED:

- small nail
- 2 foam cups
- tap water at room temperature
- a partner
- sink
- stopwatch
- notebook and pencil
- liquid cooking oil, rubbing alcohol, syrup, molasses, and soapy water

**6.** After cleaning the cup, repeat the experiment with an equal volume of another liquid at room temperature. Try cooking oil, rubbing alcohol, syrup, molasses, and soapy water.

## What's Going On?

The viscosity of liquids is similar to friction between solids. The more viscous a liquid, the slower it flows. You measured viscosity by measuring the time it took different liquids to empty from a container. You probably found that sticky molasses was the most viscous liquid (slowest to empty) and runny soapy water was the least viscous (emptied fastest).

## Keep Exploring—If You Have More Time!

- Design and carry out an experiment to see if viscosity is affected by temperature.

- Design and carry out an experiment to find out whether or not viscosity (thickness) and density are related.

stopwatch

foam cup with liquid being tested

partner

cup in sink

**Figure 5. Testing different liquids for viscosity.**

# 30 Minutes or Less

Pressed for time? Here are some experiments you can do in 30 minutes, more or less.

# 6 Density of a Liquid and a Solid

## What's the Plan?

Let's find the density of a liquid (water) and a solid (marbles).

## What You Do

1. Weigh a 100 mL graduated cylinder or a metric measuring cup. Record its mass.

2. Add 50 mL of water to the graduated cylinder (Figure 6a) or measuring cup and reweigh. Record the mass. Find the mass of the water by subtracting the mass of the cylinder or cup from the total mass you just weighed.

3. Weigh about a dozen or more dry glass marbles. Record the marbles' mass.

4. Add the marbles to the 50 mL of water. The marbles will displace a volume of water equal to their volume (Figure 6b). Record the new volume.

5. Subtract 50 mL from the volume you just recorded to find the volume of the marbles.

### WHAT YOU NEED:

- a balance
- graduated cylinder or metric measuring cup
- pen or pencil
- notebook
- water
- 1 2 or more glass marbles
- pocket calculator (optional)

**6.** From the data you have collected, calculate the density of water and the density of the marbles. Density is the mass of something divided by its volume. For example, the mass of 10 cubic centimeters ($cm^3$) of aluminum is 27 grams (g). Therefore, its density is 27 g ÷ 10 $cm^3$ = 2.7 $g/cm^3$.

## What's Going On?

You probably found the density of water to be very close to 1.0 g/mL. When the author did the experiment, he found the marbles weighed 52 g and they displaced 21 mL of water. So he found the density of the marbles to be 52 $g/21$ $cm^3$ = 2.5 $g/cm^3$. (A milliliter [mL] and a cubic centimeter [$cm^3$] have the same volume. Liquid volumes are usually measured in milliliters and solids in cubic centimeters.) Therefore, the marbles were 2.5 times as dense as the water.

## Keep Exploring—If You Have More Time!

- Find the density of other solids and liquids such as steel washers and rubbing alcohol.

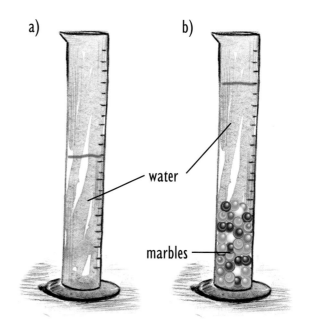

Figure 6. a) Find the mass of known volume of water. Then find its density. b) Find the volume of a known mass of marbles. Then calculate the density of the marbles.

# 7 Density of Two Liquids

## What's the Plan?

Let's find the density of water and cooking oil and then mix them.

## What You Do

1. Weigh a 100-mL graduated cylinder or a metric measuring cup. Record its mass.

2. Add 100 mL of cold water to the graduated cylinder or metric measuring cup and reweigh (Figure 7a). Record that mass.

3. Subtract the mass of the graduated cylinder or measuring cup to find the mass of the water.

4. Use your data to calculate the density of water. Record its density. Density is the mass of something divided by its volume. For example, the mass of 10 cubic centimeters ($cm^3$) of aluminum is 27 grams (g). Therefore, its density is 27 g ÷ 10 $cm^3$ = 2.7 $g/cm^3$.

5. Repeat the experiment using cooking oil in place of water.

6. Pour half the cooking oil into a drinking glass. Add 50 mL of water to the cooking oil (Figure 7b). Observe the two liquids.

> ### WHAT YOU NEED:
> - a balance
> - 100-mL graduated cylinder or a metric measuring cup
> - pen or pencil
> - notebook
> - cold water
> - cooking oil
> - drinking glass
> - calculator (optional)

## What's Going On?

You probably found the density of water to be about 1.0 g/mL. The density of cooking oil was less than 1.0 g/mL.

As you saw, the two liquids do not dissolve in one another. The less dense cooking oil floated on the more dense water. This is generally true. A less dense substance will float on a more dense substance if they don't mix.

## Keep Exploring—If You Have More Time!

- Find the density of some rubbing alcohol. Then add it to water. What happens?

- Find the density of a block of wood. Will the wood sink or float in water? Make a prediction. Then test your prediction.

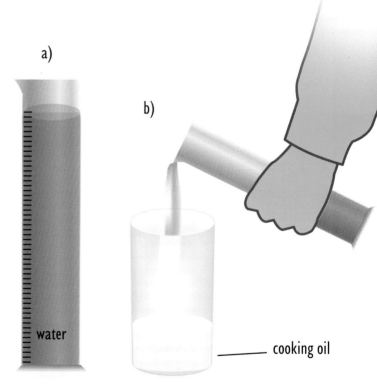

Figure 7. a) Weigh 100 mL of water in a graduated cylinder or a metric measuring cup. b) Add 50 mL of water to 50 mL of cooking oil. Do the liquids mix or remain separated?

21

# 8 Discovering with Archimedes

## What's the Plan?

Archimedes (287–212 B.C.), a Sicilian Greek mathematician and scientist, discovered an important scientific principle. You can make the same discovery.

## What You Do

1. Prepare a clay cube approximately 4 cm on a side (Figure 8a).

2. Insert a twistie into the cube. Using a spring balance, weigh the clay (Figure 8b). Record its weight.

3. Add water to a metric measuring cup (enough to submerge the clay, which you will lower into the water in step 4). Measure and record the volume of water in the cup.

4. Lower the clay, suspended from the spring balance, into the water. Be sure the clay is completely submerged but not touching the bottom of the cup (Figure 8c). Measure and record the weight of the submerged clay and the volume indicated by the water level.

5. Record the volume of water the clay displaced. Record the weight of the displaced water. (Remember: one milliliter [1 mL] of water weighs one gram [1 g].)

### WHAT YOU NEED:

- clay or plasticene
- ruler
- twistie
- spring balance 0-250 g or 0-2.5 newtons
- water
- metric measuring cup
- pen or pencil
- notebook

## What's Going On?

You probably found that the weight of the water displaced by the clay equaled or nearly equaled the weight lost by the submerged clay. If so, you have discovered Archimedes' principle—the weight of water displaced by an object immersed in the water is equal to the object's apparent loss of weight.

The author's data for this experiment was: weight of clay in air: 110 g; weight of clay in water: 50 g; clay's loss of weight in water: 60 g.

Initial volume of water: 175 mL; volume of water with clay submerged: 235 mL.

Volume of water displaced: 60 mL; weight of water displaced: 60 g.

Clay's loss of weight in water equals weight of water displaced.

## Keep Exploring—If You Have More Time!

- Show that Archimedes' principle works for other liquids, such as alcohol.

Figure 8. a) Prepare a cubic lump of clay about 4 cm on a side. b) Use a spring balance to weigh the clay. c) Submerge the clay. Find its weight in water and the weight of the water it displaces.

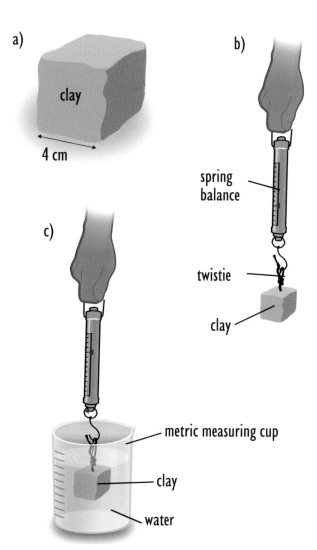

# 9 Water's Strange Behavior

## What's the Plan?

What happens to water when it freezes?

## What You Do

1. Flatten a lump of clay. Place the clay in a small jar.

2. Add several drops of food coloring to a tall water glass. Fill the glass with water.

3. Put a transparent soda straw in the glass.

4. Place your finger firmly on the top of the straw (Figure 9a).

5. Keep your finger on the straw as you lift the straw from the water. The water will stay in the straw.

6. Keeping your finger on the top of the straw, press the bottom of the straw into the lump of clay. Remove your finger from the straw. The water should remain in the straw.

7. Be sure water is not leaking from the straw. Then gently mark the water level in the straw with a marking pen. Put the jar with the water-filled straw into a freezer.

**WHAT YOU NEED:**
- clay
- small jar
- food coloring
- tall water glass
- water
- transparent soda straw
- marking pen
- a freezer
- clock or watch

**8.** After about thirty minutes, open the freezer. The water should have turned to ice. Look at the ice level in the straw (Figure 9b). Notice that the volume increased after the water froze.

## What's Going On?

If you cool most liquids to their freezing temperature, they contract as they freeze. They continue to contract as their solid state is cooled further. As a result, the density of most substances increases as the temperature decreases so that the solid is more dense than the liquid. But water, as you have seen, is different from most substances. It expands when it freezes which makes ice less dense than water. Ice floats in water.

## Keep Exploring—If You Have More Time!

- Design and do an experiment to find what happens to the density of ice as it cools below its freezing point (0°C).

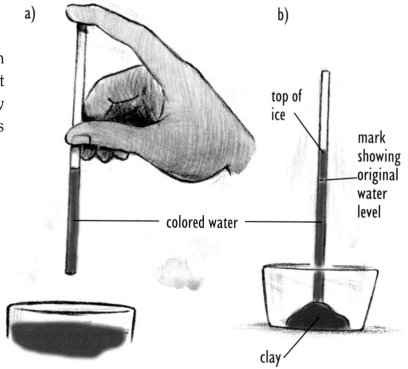

a)

b)

top of ice

mark showing original water level

colored water

clay

Figure 9. a) Partially fill a soda straw with colored water. b) What happens to the water level after the froze?

# 10 Surface Area to Volume

## What's the Plan?

How is the ratio of matter's surface area to volume affected by size?

**WHAT YOU NEED:**

- clay
- dropper
- ruler
- notebook and pencil

## What You Do

1. Make cubes from clay that are 1 cm, 2 cm, and 4 cm on a side (Figure 10).

2. Determine and record the volume of each cube.

3. Determine and record the surface area of each cube.

4. Determine and record the surface area to volume ratio for each cube.

5. Determine and record the weight to surface area ratio for each cube. Remember, doubling the volume doubles the weight.

## What's Going On?

Table 1 should summarize your findings.

As you can see, bigger cubes have less surface area per volume and per weight than smaller cubes. This is true in general. A baby has to be kept warm. Its surface area to volume is so large that it loses heat rapidly to its surroundings. An adult loses heat less rapidly because the surface area to volume is smaller.

| Table 1: Surface area to volume and surface area to weight ratios for cubes of different dimensions | | | | |
|---|---|---|---|---|
| Length of cube (cm) | Volume of cube (cm³) | Surface area of cube (cm²) | Surface area to volume (cm²/cm³) | Surface area to weight (cm²/g) |
| 1 | 1 | 6 | 6:1 | 6:1 |
| 2 | 8 | 24 | 3:1 | 3:1 |
| 4 | 64 | 96 | 3:2 | 3:2 |

## Keep Exploring—If You Have More Time!

- Use equal volumes of water to make an ice cube and a pancake-shaped piece of ice. Place both in a pail of water. Predict which one will melt first. Were you right? Explain why.

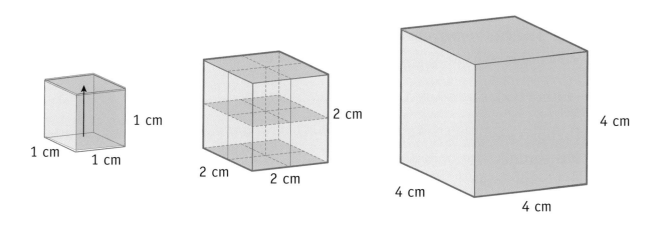

Figure 10. Make cubes of clay that are 1 cm, 2 cm, and 4 cm on a side. Find the volumes and surface areas of these cubes. Then calculate their surface area to volume ratios.

# 15 Minutes or Less

Time is really in short supply if you need an experiment you can do in 15 minutes. Here to rescue you are more experiments you can do that quickly.

# 11 Thermal (Heat) Expansion of a Gas

## What's the Plan?

What happens when we heat and cool a gas (air)?

> **WHAT YOU NEED:**
> - round balloon
> - 2-liter plastic soda bottle
> - hot water faucet
> - refrigerator
> - clock

## What You Do

1. Blow up a balloon several times so it expands easily. Then pull the neck of the balloon over the mouth of an empty 2-liter plastic soda bottle.

2. Hold the bottle under a hot water faucet (Figure 11). The hot water will heat the air in the bottle. Watch the balloon as the gas in the bottle expands.

3. Put the balloon-covered bottle in a refrigerator. Leave it for 10 minutes.

4. Remove the bottle from the refrigerator. You will see that the air's volume has shrunk. The balloon collapsed and may even have been drawn into the bottle.

## What's Going On?

All gases expand when heated. In fact, all gases at 0°C expand by the same fraction of their volume (1/273) for each Celsius degree increase in temperature. As Table 2 shows, this is not true of solids.

| Table 2: Increase in length of 1.0-m-long rods of different solids after a temperature increase of 100°C | | | |
|---|---|---|---|
| Solid | Increase in length (mm) | Solid | Increase in length (mm) |
| aluminum | 2.5 | iron | 1.1 |
| brass | 1.8 | platinum | 0.9 |
| copper | 1.7 | silver | 1.8 |
| glass | 1.7 | quartz | 0.04 |
| gold | 1.4 | glass (pyrex) | 0.3 |

## Keep Exploring—If You Have More Time!

- Place the mouth of a rigid plastic or glass bottle under the surface of some water in a basin. Heat the air in the bottle by covering the bottle with a cloth soaked in hot water. What evidence do you have that a gas expands when heated?

- Keep the mouth of the bottle under the water. Cover the bottle with a cloth soaked in ice water. What evidence do you have that a gas contracts when cooled?

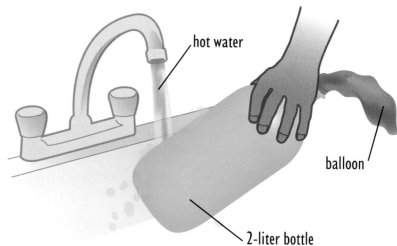
hot water

balloon

2-liter bottle

Figure 11. Pull the neck of a balloon over the mouth of a 2-liter soda bottle. Let hot water flow over the bottle. What happens to the balloon?

29

# 12 Diffusion of Fluids

## What's the Plan?

Diffusion is the random motion of molecules that causes a substance to spread from a region of high concentration to one with a lower concentration. Let's look for diffusion in fluids (gases and liquids).

## What You Do

**WHAT YOU NEED:**

- pen or pencil
- notebook
- bottle of ammonia or perfume
- clock or watch
- 2 vials or small, clear drinking glasses
- cold water
- hot water
- food coloring

1. Place a fresh bottle of ammonia or a bottle of perfume on a table.

2. Record the time. Then immediately open the bottle and walk three feet away. How much time passes before you smell the ammonia or perfume?

3. Seal the ammonia or perfume bottle and put it away.

4. Nearly fill one vial or small, clear drinking glass with very cold water. Nearly fill a second identical vial or glass with hot water.

5. Add one drop of the same food coloring to both the hot and the cold water (Figure 12). Watch the color diffuse (spread out) in the water.

## What's Going On?

You probably smelled the ammonia or perfume after a few minutes. This meant that molecules had diffused through the air during that time and finally reached your nostrils.

By watching the food coloring diffuse, you could see that it spread faster in the hot water. The reason is that the speed of molecules is related to temperature. Molecules move faster at higher temperatures.

## Keep Exploring—If You Have More Time!

- It probably took the ammonia or perfume molecules several minutes to travel the few feet to your nose. Yet we know that air molecules at room temperature move at an average speed of about 500 m/s (1,100 mph). Why did it take the gas so long to travel such a short distance? (Hint: There are 25 million trillion air molecules per cubic centimeter of air.)

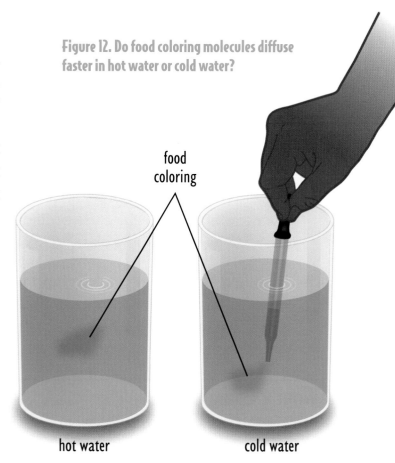

Figure 12. Do food coloring molecules diffuse faster in hot water or cold water?

food coloring

hot water          cold water

# 13 Climbing Liquids

## What's the Plan?

Does water hold together well enough to "climb" up narrow spaces?

## What You Do

1. Look at the photograph in Figure 13a. It shows that water will "climb" up narrow tubes.

2. Tear off a piece of paper towel. Look at it closely with a magnifying glass. See the tiny wood fibers. They are packed so close together that they form narrow tubes.

**WHAT YOU NEED:**
- paper towel
- magnifying glass
- water
- food coloring
- saucer
- shallow dish
- 2 drinking glasses with straight sides

3. Add a drop of food coloring and a few drops of water to a saucer. Place the edge of the paper towel against the colored water. With a magnifying glass, watch the water move between the fibers.

4. Put a few drops of food coloring in a pie tin or other shallow dish or container. Add some water. Then put two drinking glasses with straight sides in the water. Bring the sides of the glasses very close together (Figure 13b). Watch the water "climb" up the narrow space between the glasses.

## What's Going On?

Water is attracted to glass, wood, and other solids. It adheres to them. Water is also strongly attracted to itself; it is cohesive. These forces are strong enough to overcome gravity in narrow spaces where the weight of the water

is small. As a result, water will move up narrow spaces if it is attracted to their walls.

Water's cohesiveness is the result of its polar molecules (Figure 13c). One side of a water molecule is slightly positive. Its other side is slightly negative. This polarity causes water molecules to attract one another, which makes water hold together very well.

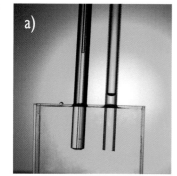

## Keep Exploring—If You Have More Time!

- Hang identical, long, narrow strips of paper towel in different liquids. Use colored water as a standard and compare it with such liquids as rubbing alcohol, cooking oil, vinegar, salt water, and soapy water. Do different liquids ascend to different heights?

- Does the width of the paper have any effect on the height to which water will rise? If it does, can you explain why?

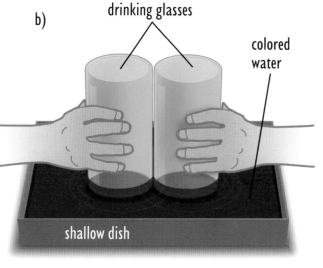

Figure 13. a) Water will "climb" up narrow spaces, a phenomenon known as capillarity. b) Put two glasses close together in some shallow water. Watch the water move up the narrow space between the glasses. c) Water molecules are polar. This causes them to attract one another. It accounts for water's cohesiveness.

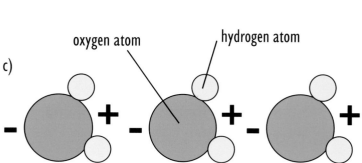

# 14 The Volume of One Drop

## What's the Plan?

Can you find the volume of a single drop of water?

## What You Do

1. Place a small graduated cylinder or a medicine cup near a sink.

2. Fill a drinking glass with cold water.

3. Use an eyedropper to add the water drop by drop to the graduated cylinder or medicine cup (Figure 14). Count the drops as you add them until you fill the cylinder or medicine cup. Record the number of drops you added.

4. Divide the total volume of water by the number of drops you added. The result is the volume of one drop.

## What's Going On?

You measured the volume of a drop by what is called an indirect method. You assumed that all the drops had the same volume, which is a reasonable thing to do.

**WHAT YOU NEED:**

- graduated cylinder (if possible choose one with a 10-mL capacity) or a medicine cup

- sink

- drinking glass

- cold water

- pen or pencil

- notebook

- eyedropper

- calculator (optional)

If you found, as the author did, that it took 205 drops to accumulate 10 mL of water, then the volume of one drop is:

$$\frac{10.0 \text{ mL}}{205 \text{ drops}} = 0.0488 \text{ mL.}$$

## Keep Exploring—If You Have More Time!

- Does one drop of hot water have the same volume as one drop of cold water?

- Find the volume of one drop of the following liquids: rubbing alcohol, soapy water, and salad oil. How do they compare with water?

- Find the mass of one grain of sand.

- Find the volume of one grain of sand.

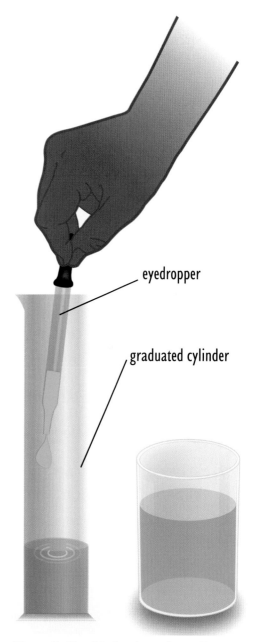

eyedropper

graduated cylinder

Figure 14. How big is a drop of water?

35

# 5 Minutes or Less

Are you desperate? Do you have very little time to prepare a project? If so, you have come to the right place. Here are experiments you can do in five minutes or less.

# 15 Weighing Air

## What's the Plan?

Can you weigh air?

## What You Do

**WHAT YOU NEED:**
- a balance
- plastic trash bag
- twistie
- pen or pencil
- notebook

**1.** Use a balance to weigh an empty, flattened, plastic kitchen trash bag and a twistie that will be used to seal the bag. Record the weight of the bag and twistie.

**2.** Drag the bag through air to fill it with the gas (Figure 15a).

**3.** Seal the air-filled bag using the twistie.

**4.** Reweigh the bag and twistie now that the bag has been filled with air (Figure 15b). Record that weight.

## What's Going On?

You probably found that the air-filled bag and the empty bag had the same weight. Does that mean air is weightless?

Suppose you pumped the air out of a rigid metal container to create a vacuum. If you weighed the empty container, let air back in, and then reweighed it, you would find that air does have weight. In fact, one liter of air weighs approximately 1.2 grams at normal air pressure and room temperature.

It appeared to be weightless in your experiment because any object weighed in air is buoyed upward (lifted) by a force equal to the weight of the air it displaces. This is known as Archimedes' principle (see Experiment 8). A volume of air weighed in air is buoyed upward by its own weight so it appears to be weightless.

## Keep Exploring—If You Have More Time!

- To see that air really does have weight, let all the air out of a soccer ball or a football. Weigh the deflated ball. Then pump air into it until it reaches regulation pressure or feels very firm. Then reweigh the ball. Has its weight increased?

- Figure out a way to weigh other gases such as carbon dioxide and helium by taking Archimedes' principle into account. (Remember, a liter of air weighs 1.2 grams.)

a)

plastic bag

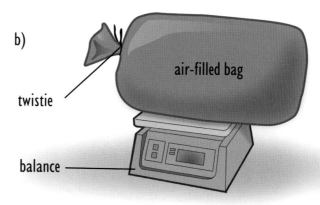

b)

twistie

air-filled bag

balance

Figure 15. a) Fill an open kitchen trash bag by dragging it through air. b) Reweigh the air-filled bag and twistie.

# 16 Water Sticks Together

## What's the Plan?

How well does water hold together?

## What You Do

**WHAT YOU NEED:**
- steel paper clip
- cup
- water
- dinner fork
- bar of soap

**1.** Drop a steel paper clip into a cup of water. The paper clip sinks because steel, with a density of 7.9 $g/cm^3$, is more dense than water. Water's density is 1.0 $g/cm^3$.

**2.** Now rinse the cup thoroughly with water in case any soap film remains on it.

**3.** Fill the cup with cold water. Then, using a dinner fork, gently place the paper clip on the water's surface (Figure 16a). The paper clip floats, giving the water a dimpled surface (Figure 16b).

**4.** Touch the water with a bar of soap. The paper clip sinks.

## What's Going On?

Because they are polar, water molecules attract one another. (Look back at Figure 13c.) This attraction causes water to hold together very well. Water molecules below the surface are attracted equally in all directions (Figure 16c). But water molecules on the surface are pulled inward by the molecules beneath them. This gives water a skin-like surface, which is known as surface tension. Adding even very small amounts of soap reduces surface tension. The soap molecules get between the water molecules and greatly reduce the attractive forces between the water molecules.

# Keep Exploring—If You Have More Time!

- Design and conduct an experiment to measure the surface tension of water as well as other liquids such as rubbing alcohol and soapy water.

- See how many drops of water you can place on a penny. How does this experiment show that water holds together very well?

a)

Figure 16. a) Gently place a paper clip on the surface of some water in a cup. b) The photograph shows a paper clip floating on water. c) Water molecules within water are attracted equally in all directions. Molecules on the surface are pulled inward giving the water a skin-like cover.

clean water

b)

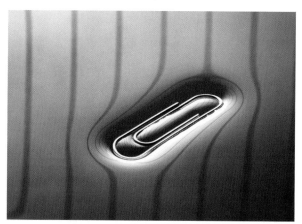

c)

surface molecule

submerged molecule

# 17 Liquid Expansion and Temperature

## What's the Plan?

What happens to the volume of a liquid when its temperature changes?

**WHAT YOU NEED:**

- alcohol-based thermometer
- ice cube

## What You Do

**1.** Put your warm thumb on the bulb of a household thermometer (Figure 17a). Watch the liquid rise as it expands.

**2.** Put an ice cube on the bulb of the thermometer (Figure 17b). Watch the volume of the liquid decrease.

## What's Going On?

As you saw, a liquid expands (its volume increases) when its temperature rises. Warm molecules move faster than cold molecules and take up more space. A liquid shrinks (its volume decreases) when its temperature is reduced because cold molecules move slower and take up less space. The amount

| Table 3: Expansion, in milliliters (mL), of one liter (L) of liquid per degree Celsius temperature increase ||
|---|---|
| Liquid | Expansion (mL/°C) |
| ethanol | 0.75 |
| carbon disulfide | 1.15 |
| glycerin | 0.49 |
| mercury | 0.18 |
| water | 0.45 |

that the volume changes with temperature is different for different liquids. Table 3 indicates the increase in volume of 1.0 liter of several different liquids per degree change in Celsius temperature.

## Keep Exploring—If You Have More Time!

- Use what you have learned to make a simple thermometer from colored water, a test tube, clay, and a soda straw.

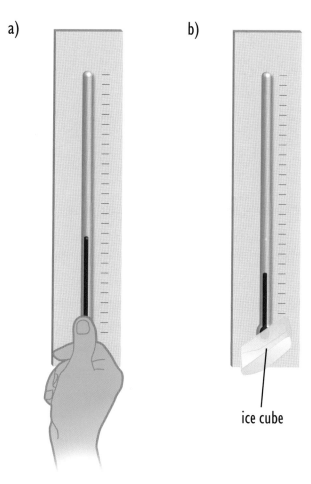

a)

b)

ice cube

**Figure 17. a) Put your thumb on the bulb of a thermometer. Watch the volume of the liquid in the thermometer expand. b) Put an ice cube on the bulb of a thermometer. Watch the volume of the liquid in the thermometer shrink.**

# 18 Metal Expansion When Heated

## What's the Plan?

Can you use heat to loosen a tight-fitting metal jar cap?

**WHAT YOU NEED:**

- glass jar with a metal screw-on cap
- hot water faucet

## What You Do

**1.** Find a glass jar with a metal screw-on cap.

**2.** Tighten the lid so that the jar is very difficult to open.

**3.** Hold the tight jar lid under a stream of hot water from a faucet for 20 seconds (Figure 18). Try to keep the hot water on the metal and off the glass.

**4.** After heating the jar cap with hot water, open the jar again.

## What's Going On?

You probably found the jar was easier to open after you held it in hot water. The reason it was easier to open than before was because the metal lid expanded slightly when it was heated. In addition, the metal is a good conductor of heat while the glass is a poor conductor. The heat spread throughout the metal cap, but little heat was conducted into the glass, which will also expand when its temperature rises.

## Keep Exploring—If You Have More Time!

- Design and do an experiment to compare the expansion of different metals, such as steel, aluminum, copper, zinc, lead, etc., over the same increase in temperature.

- Design and do an experiment to compare the ability of different metals, such as steel, aluminum, copper, zinc, lead, etc., to conduct heat.

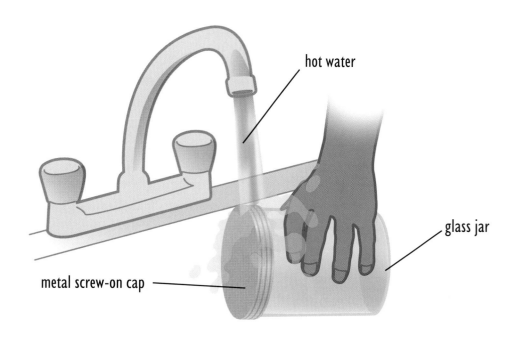

hot water

glass jar

metal screw-on cap

**Figure 18. Metal expands when heated.**

# Words to Know

**Archimedes**—An early Greek scientist (287–212 B.C.) who discovered a principle that now bears his name.

**Archimedes' principle**—An object placed in a fluid will be buoyed up by a force equal to the weight of the fluid displaced.

**cohesion**—The attractive forces between molecules of the same substance. For example, water molecules are attracted to one another.

**density**—The mass of a substance divided by its volume. The density of water is one gram per milliliter or one gram per cubic centimeter. A milliliter and a cubic centimeter have the same volume. Gases have small densities because their molecules are far apart.

**diffusion**—The random motion of molecules of a gas or liquid that causes it to spread out in its surrounding space.

**electrical conductivity**—The ability of a substance to conduct electricity (electrons). Metals are generally good electrical conductors.

**gas**—A state of matter that has neither a definite volume nor a definite shape.

**liquid**—A state of matter that can't be compressed. Liquids have a definite volume but they take the shape of the container in which they are placed.

**solid**—A state of matter that has both a definite shape and volume.

**states of matter**—The three states in which matter exists are solids, liquids, and gases. A fourth state, plasmas, is beyond the scope of this book.

**surface area to volume**—The ratio of an object's surface area to its volume. In general, the larger an object, the smaller its surface area to volume.

**surface tension**—Molecules below the surface of a liquid are attracted equally in all directions, but molecules on the surface are pulled inward by the molecules beneath them. As a result of these cohesive forces between molecules, liquid surfaces tend to behave as if they had a skin.

**thermal expansion**—The expansion of a solid, liquid, or gas when its temperature increases. All gases expand equally when heated, Different liquids and solids vary in their expansion when heated.

**viscosity**—The resistance of a liquid to flow. The more viscous a liquid, the slower it flows.

**volume**—The amount of space occupied by a solid, liquid, or gas.

**weight**—Earth's gravitational force on a sample of matter.

# Further Reading

## Books

Bailey, Jacqui. *How Can Solids Be Changed?* Mankato, Minn.: Smart Apple Media, 2007.

Bardhan-Quallen, Sudipta. *Championship Science Fair Projects: 100 Sure-To-Win Experiments*. New York: Scholastic, 2005.

Claybourne, Anna. *The Science of a Glass of Water: The Science of States of Matter*. New York: Gareth Stevens Publishing, 2009.

Dicker, Katie. *Properties of Matter*. New York: Windmill Books, 2011

DiSpezio, Michael A. *Super Sensational Science Fair Projects*. New York: Sterling Publishers, 2004.

Farndon, John. *Solids, Liquids, and Gases*. New York: Benchmark Books, 2009.

Rhatigan, Joe, and Rain Newcomb. *Prize-Winning Science Fair Projects for Curious Kids*. New York: Lark Books, 2006.

Riley, Peter D. *All About Gases*. Mankato, Minn.: Smart Apple Media, 2007.

Solway, Andrew. *The Science of a Loaf of Bread: The Science of Changing Properties*. New York: Gareth Stevens Publishers, 2009.

# Internet Addresses

Galaxy.net. Solids, Liquids, and Gases.
<http://www.galaxy.net/~k12/phases/>

Science Kids. Physics Science Fair Projects.
<http://www.sciencekids.co.nz/projects/physics.html>

# Index